Salaryman Secrets!

I Talk You Talk Press

CONTENTS

SALARYMAN SECRETS

Workers in Japan share their embarrassing work stories!

Salaryman is a Japanese/English word. It means "business man" or "office worker".

ONE

Kazu (39)

I work at a large company in Tokyo. I have a very hard job, and sometimes I have to work until 11 or 12 at night.

One night, I was working alone in the office. It was 10:00pm. I was very tired and very hungry. I wanted to go home, but I couldn't. I had a lot of work. So I went to a convenience store to buy a rice ball. I was walking to the rice ball section, when I saw the beer in the refrigerator. Of course, we cannot drink beer at work, but it was late, I was alone in the office and I was very thirsty. The beer looked delicious. So, I bought a can of beer.

I went back to the office and started eating the rice ball. I opened the can of beer and drank a little. Then, I heard a noise at the door. The door opened and my boss walked into the office! I was very surprised. I quickly put the can of beer under my desk.

He walked over to my desk and said, "I left some documents here. I need to read them before tomorrow morning."

My boss picked up the documents and put them in his bag. Then, he went home.

I looked under my desk for my can of beer. The beer was all over the floor! When my boss came to my desk I was very nervous and my foot kicked the beer can! The carpet was very wet and very smelly. I cleaned the carpet. It took ten minutes to clean. Then I finished my work and went home at 11:30pm.

The next morning, I arrived at the office at 8:20am. Some of my co-workers were already in the office. They were talking about something. I said, "What are you talking about?"

One of my co-workers said, "There is a strange smell in this office. It smells like old beer!"

I said, "Really? I can't smell anything!"

TWO

Shingo (34)

I am a graphic designer. I live in a small town. Many of my clients are companies in the same town. I often design pamphlets for two private English schools in the town. I designed a new pamphlet for one of the schools. Of course, the design and pamphlet details are secret. I finished the pamphlet design and I emailed a PDF file to the school.

However, I made a very big mistake. I emailed it to the other school - the rival school!

I didn't realize my mistake until I called the school.

I said, "Do you like the design?"

The school owner said, "I haven't seen the design yet. Please send it."

I said, "I sent it by email an hour ago."

The owner said, "I haven't received it yet."

When I checked my email outbox, I was very shocked. I called both schools and apologized many times. Of course, the owners of both schools were very angry.

They said, "Why didn't you check the email BEFORE you sent it? You have to be more careful!"

After that, both schools stopped asking me to design their pamphlets. They don't trust me anymore. I lost TWO customers. Now, when I send emails, I am very careful.

THREE

Greg (26) (An American man working in Japan)

I teach English at a large English school in Osaka. Our language school teaches English, Chinese, Korean, French, Italian and German.

One day, a man came to the school. He wanted to study Italian. The manager of my school arranged a trial lesson with Marco, the Italian teacher. The man's trial lesson was at 9:00am on Monday morning.

However, that day, Marco didn't come to work. The man arrived for his lesson, but there was no teacher! The manager of my school was panicking.

She said, "Marco is not here! But the man came for a lesson! What should I do?"

I wanted to help the manager. So I thought about the problem. When I was at university, I had an Italian friend. He taught me some Italian words, so I could understand very basic Italian.

I thought, *Not many Japanese people speak Italian. So the man will be a beginner. I can pretend to be Italian and I can teach him a very basic lesson. I can teach him "hello", "how are you", "please", "thank you" and "goodbye".*

So, I said to the manager, "I can speak a little Italian. I can teach the trial lesson."

She was very happy. She said, "Thank you so much!"

I went to the classroom. I had a very big shock.

The man had lived in Italy for five years, and he could speak Italian very well! He was almost native level! I could only say "hello", "how are you", "please", "thank you" and "goodbye"! He started

5

talking to me in Italian about Italian movies. I didn't understand anything!

Of course, the man was very angry and did not stay for the lesson. And the manager was very angry with me too!

FOUR

Chiharu (29)

I work in an office in Tokyo. My company has a text messaging system. We can send text messages to other workers in the office from our computers.

My friend and I always used this messaging system to talk in the office. We talked about many things, such as our work or our weekends. Sometimes, we talked about our co-workers!

One day, I was text messaging one of my friends in the office. I was complaining about our boss. I wrote many bad things about our boss.

I wrote "I want to see my boyfriend on Sunday, so I asked the manager, Mr Matsuura, for a holiday. He said, 'No! You have to work on Sunday!' He is very unkind. I hate him."

I sent the message to my friend's computer. She read it, and then she wrote a reply. Then, she made a big mistake.

She pressed "Send all" instead of "Send".

The message went to all the computers in the company! All the workers received the message! She quickly sent another message to all the workers. She wrote "Please do not read that last message! Please delete it!"

Luckily, our boss was in a meeting at that time. I went to his office. His computer was on. So, I deleted the message from my boss's computer. He didn't see the message, but many other people did. I was really embarrassed! Now, I never send private messages on the messaging system! It's too dangerous!

FIVE

Keita (36)
I work in the head office of a very large company in Tokyo.

Every April, new employees join the company.

On the first day, they have an orientation session in the large meeting hall. The assistant-manager of each section of the company gives a presentation about their section. I am the assistant manager of the HR section, so I have to give a presentation to the new employees about the HR section.

I always get very nervous before presentations or speeches. I really don't like public speaking.

Last year, at the orientation session, just before the presentation, I got stomach-ache. I needed to go to the toilet, but I didn't have time. I walked on stage and gave the presentation. I made a few mistakes, but it was fine. The new employees listened very carefully.

After my speech, there was a ten-minute break. In the break, the new employees sat very quietly in their chairs. They didn't go to the coffee machine or go to the smoking room. I think they were all very nervous.

At that time, I had very bad stomach-ache. I needed to go to the toilet. I finished my presentation and then I went to the toilet. I had diarrhoea. I sometimes get diarrhoea when I am nervous.

When I came out of the toilets I went back into the meeting hall. The room was quiet. Everyone was looking at me. Then, I realized. The microphone on my jacket was on! Everyone in the room heard me in the toilet! I was so embarrassed! My co-workers didn't say anything, but my boss did not look happy. Now, when I finish presentations, I always check my microphone. I always switch it OFF!

SIX

Naho (25)

Last year, I was a new employee at my company. I had to answer the phone every day. It was always very busy and there were many phone calls every day.

One day, I answered the phone. The caller was Mr Asada, the president of another company. Mr Asada, and the president of my company, Mr Itagaki, had a plan to have lunch at a very expensive hotel restaurant the next day.

Mr Asada said, "I am sorry. I cannot meet Mr Itagaki tomorrow. I have to cancel our lunch meeting. Please tell him. I am very sorry. I will call him soon."

I said "OK, Mr Asada. I will tell him. Thank you for calling."

Then, three seconds later, another phone call came, and then another call, and then another…I was very busy. I forgot to tell Mr Itagaki about the call from Mr Asada!

So, the next day, Mr Itagaki went to lunch at the hotel. He waited for Mr Asada for a long time. Then, he called Mr Asada on his mobile phone.

Mr Asada said, "I called your office yesterday. I spoke to a secretary in your office. I cancelled the lunch meeting."

Mr Itagaki came back to the office.

He said to me, "Why didn't you give me the message from Mr. Asada? I waited in the hotel restaurant for thirty minutes! I had to pay for lunch for two people! It was very expensive! You must be more careful!"

Now, I am always very careful! When I get a message for Mr Itagaki, I always write it on a memo pad!

SEVEN

Yoshi (32)

I work for a large company in Tokyo. My office is very busy, and I always have a lot of work to do. I usually stay at the office until 9 or 10:00pm. One day, I was very busy. I had to read some documents for an important presentation the next morning. I looked at the office clock. It was 10:00pm. I was very tired and hungry. I decided to go home, have dinner and read the documents at home. I put the documents and files in a bag. I had two bags. One was my briefcase, and one was the bag of documents. Some of the documents were very private. They were about our company's future. I got home, had dinner and then I worked until 2:00am. I was very sleepy.

The next morning, I woke up at 6:30am, drank some coffee and then went to catch the train. On the train, I was very sleepy. I got off the train and started walking to my office. Then I thought, *The documents! Where is the bag of documents?*

I didn't have the bag of documents! I ran to the station office and told one of the station employees. He called someone. I was very worried. I looked at my watch. It was 8:15. I had to prepare for the presentation at 9:00! The station man said, "The train conductor found your bag. He gave the package to the station office at the next station."

I had two choices. 1. Go to work without the private documents, and arrive before 9:00, or 2. Get a taxi to the next station, get the documents and be late for work. Of course, I chose number 2. I called my boss and said "I got up late. I'm sorry, I will be ten minutes late for the meeting."

Then, I got a taxi to the next station, picked up my bag of documents from the station office and took the taxi to my office.

Of course, my boss was very angry because everyone was waiting for me, but if I said "I'm sorry, I took the private documents home, and then I left them on a train", he would be very angry. And of course, I would lose my job!

EIGHT

Nana (27)

One day, I woke up with a cold and a fever.

I called the office and said, "I have a cold, so this morning I will go to the hospital and get some medicine. I will come to the office at 11:00am."

My section manager said, "OK, take care. See you later."

Then, I went to the hospital. There were not many people in the hospital, and I saw the doctor very quickly.

He said, "You have a cold. I will give you some medicine."

I was in the hospital for around fifteen minutes.

Then, I went to the pharmacy and got the medicine. I looked at my watch. It was 9:30. I had two choices: 1) Go to the office, or 2) Relax and go to the office at 11:00am.

I decided to relax and go to the office at 11:00am.

So, I went to a coffee shop. I drank cocoa. In the coffee shop, I saw my friend. We started talking. We had a good time, talking and laughing. I always feel better when I drink cocoa and see my friend.

Then, I looked out of the window. My section manager was outside the coffee shop! Then, he walked into the coffee shop! I was very shocked.

I put my hat on and pulled my scarf around my face, but he saw me! I looked at him and he looked at me.

He didn't say anything, but I'm sure he was thinking: *She doesn't look sick. Why is she in a coffee shop with her friend? Why isn't she in the office?*

However, I was thinking: *Why is my section manager here in the coffee*

shop? Why isn't he in the office?
    We didn't say anything about it when we went back to the office!

NINE

Brad (31)

I work in a small translation company in Japan. I joined the company three years ago. My native language is English, but I can also speak Japanese. In the office, I check translations and send them to the clients. Then, at the end of each month, I send invoices to my clients.

When I joined the company, I was very nervous. I didn't understand my job very well. One of my co-workers, Miho, was very kind. She helped me a lot.

In my second month at the office, I made a big mistake.

My company did a very large translation for a big food company in Japan. I checked the translation. Then, I sent it to the food company. At the end of the month, I had to write an invoice.

I asked Miho, "How much should I write on this invoice?"

She said, "ni-jyu-man yen". This is "two hundred thousand yen" in Japanese. (200,000).

However, I made a mistake.

I wrote "ni-man yen". This is "twenty thousand yen" in Japanese. (20,000).

Then, I sent the invoice.

A few days later, Miho checked the invoices.

She said, "What's this?! It's not twenty thousand yen! It's two hundred thousand yen!"

I looked at the invoice. I said, "Oh no! I am so sorry! What should I do?"

She said, "You must call the food company. You must apologize!"

So I called the food company. I was very nervous. I said, "I'm very sorry. I made a mistake."

Then, I had to send a new invoice. I was really embarrassed. Luckily, Miho is very kind. She didn't tell our boss. Now, I always check the numbers and invoices very carefully before I send them!

TEN

Kotaro (26)

I work for a pharmaceutical company in western Japan. I am a salesman. I sell medicine to hospitals and clinics.

I started working at the company three years ago when I was twenty-three. Of course, I was very nervous. I wanted to make a good impression.

When I started working, I had to visit hospitals, clinics and pharmacies every day. I talked to doctors and hospital owners about my company's medicine. Many of the hospitals were very far from my office, so I had to use the company car.

The company car was small, but it was new. I liked driving the car.

One Friday afternoon, I went to a small clinic, to sell some medicine. The clinic was in the countryside. It took two hours to get to the clinic from my office. The roads near the clinic were very narrow. There were many rice fields around the clinic. There was a small rice field in front of the clinic car park.

I had a long meeting with the owner of the hospital. We talked for around two hours.

The meeting finished at 5pm. I went out to the car park. It was raining heavily, and the sky was very grey. I got into my car. The car park was very small and difficult to enter and exit.

I drove out of the car park. I couldn't see very well. The front windscreen of the car was very misty.

Suddenly the car fell down. There was a large noise.

I shouted, "Oh no!"

I was in the rice field! I crashed the car into the rice field! The rice field was one metre lower than the road. The front of the car was in the mud. The back of the car was in the air. I couldn't move! I couldn't get out of the car! I panicked.

Luckily, the owner of the hospital saw me. He called the rescue service. The rescue service pulled my car out of the rice field. There was a little damage to the front of the car. It was only my fourth week at the company. I didn't want to tell my boss or my co-workers, so I drove to a car garage. I asked the mechanic to repair the damage.

He looked at the car and said, "OK. It will cost eighty thousand yen. I can do it tomorrow." (Eighty thousand yen is about a thousand US dollars.)

I said, "OK. Please repair it."

I stayed in a hotel that night. Then, the next day, the mechanic repaired my car.

I paid the eighty thousand yen. At that time, my salary was not so high. It was very expensive for me.

On Monday morning, my manager said, "How was the meeting with the hospital owner on Friday?"

I said, "Oh, it was good."

He said, "The weather was very bad on Friday. I was worried about you. The roads near the hospital are very narrow."

I said, "Oh, it was no problem. I drove very slowly and carefully."

He said, "You are a good employee. You are very careful."

I said, "Thank you."

I hope he doesn't find out the truth!

THANK YOU

Thank you for reading Salaryman Secrets! We hope you enjoyed it. (Word count: 3,166)

If you would like to read more graded readers, please visit our website
http://www.italkyoutalk.com

Other Level 2 graded readers include
Adventure in Rome
Andre's Dream
A Passion for Music
Christmas Tales
Danger in Seattle
Don't Come Back
Finders Keepers…
Marcy's Bakery
Men's Konkatsu Tales
Stories for Halloween
The Perfect Wedding
The House in the Forest
The School on Bolt Street
Train Travel
Trouble in Paris
Women's Konkatsu Tales

ABOUT THE AUTHOR

I Talk You Talk Press is a Japan-based publisher of language textbooks, graded readers and language learning/teaching resources.

Our team is made up of highly experienced language teachers and translators, who have all studied at least one additional language to an advanced level.

This experience enables us to design our materials from the perspective of both the teacher and the learner. We consult with both teachers and language learners when designing our textbooks and graded readers, and test our materials extensively in the classroom before publication.

We are a fast-growing press, and currently publish graded readers for learners of English. We publish new graded readers monthly.

www.ingramcontent.com/pod-product-compliance
Lightning Source LLC
Chambersburg PA
CBHW022353040426
42449CB00006B/852